In the post

Ruth Thomson

Photographs by Maggie Murray
Illustrations by Sheila Jackson

A & C Black · London

A CIP catalogue record for this book is available
from the British Library

ISBN 0–7136–3184–8

First published 1990 by A & C Black (Publishers) Ltd
35 Bedford Row, London WC1R 4JH

Filmset by August Filmsetting, Haydock, St Helens
Printed in Belgium by Proost International Book Production

Acknowledgements

The author and publisher would like to thank the following
people for loaning items from their collections for photography
– Philip Poole, 'His Nibs'; Maurice Rickards, President of the
Ephemera Society; Peter and Alison Walton. They would also
like to thank Jean Ferrugia, Post Office archivist, Maureen
Greenland of the Writing Equipment Society, Douglas Muir
and Tony Gammons of the National Postal Museum, Peter
Howe of the Post Office Photographic Service, Gill Tanner and
A.J. Ward for their helpful advice and comments. Thanks are
also due to Rachel Wright for her invaluable research

Photographs by Maggie Murray except for: p3, 24 Beamish
Open Air Museum; p4 The Hulton Deutsch Picture Library;
p14(bottom), 15, 16, 17, 20, 21, 23, 25, 26, 28 Post Office
14(top), 16(bottom right), 18, 22 Crown Copyright; Copyright
p27 The Daily Graphic; Cover (inset) Crown Copyright

Source of quotes

p 24/25 Lark Rise to Candleford, Flora Thompson
published Penguin Books 1973 (*pages 394 and 405*)
p 18 Destiny Obscure, ed. John Burnett
published Allen Lane, 1982 (*page 120 Edith Hall*)

Contents

Letter writing

When you want to get in touch with a friend or relative, you can make a phone call or send a letter or a card. People who work in offices might use a fax machine, telex or computer terminal to send messages quickly.

At the turn of the century, sending letters was the only way most people could stay in contact with friends, relatives and clients. Telegrams were used mainly for sending urgent news that couldn't wait for the post. The expensive, newly-invented telephone system was used only by businesses and the wealthy.

▲ Sturdy wooden writing boxes like this were useful for travellers and for people living overseas. More dainty writing boxes were used at home.

Well-off ladies had their own writing desks, ▶ with drawers and shelves at the back for stationery and their letters.

After 1870, when schooling was made compulsory, more people learned to read and write. Letter writing became popular with ordinary working people and several books were published with hints on:

'The proper manner of sending a letter to assist those who are totally inexperienced in such matters.'

▼ Letterwriting manuals provided dozens of model letters on the correct way to write accepting or refusing an invitation, announcing a death, asking for a job, engaging a servant or even accepting an offer of marriage.

The Young Woman's Companion gave this advice:

'Avoid using unmeaning or vulgar phrases, as '*You know*,' '*You see.*' Use good paper. See that it is clean. Fold your letter neatly. These apparent trifles should be attended to, as many persons judge of a writer's character and habits by the appearance of his letter.'

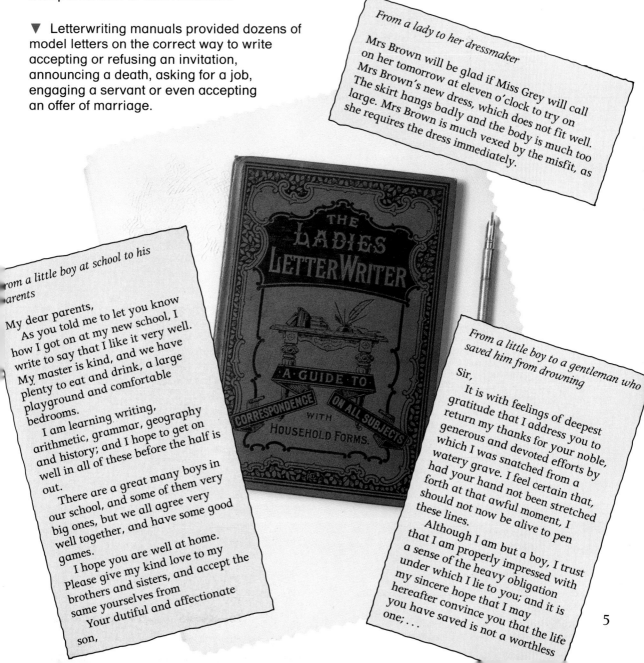

From a lady to her dressmaker

Mrs Brown will be glad if Miss Grey will call on her tomorrow at eleven o'clock to try on Mrs Brown's new dress, which does not fit well. The skirt hangs badly and the body is much too large. Mrs Brown is much vexed by the misfit, as she requires the dress immediately.

From a little boy at school to his parents

My dear parents,
As you told me to let you know how I got on at my new school, I write to say that I like it very well. My master is kind, and we have plenty to eat and drink, a large playground and comfortable bedrooms.
I am learning writing, arithmetic, grammar, geography and history; and I hope to get on well in all of these before the half is out.
There are a great many boys in our school, and some of them very big ones, but we all agree very well together, and have some good games.
I hope you are well at home. Please give my kind love to my brothers and sisters, and accept the same yourselves from
Your dutiful and affectionate son,

From a little boy to a gentleman who saved him from drowning

Sir,
It is with feelings of deepest gratitude that I address you to return my thanks for your noble, generous and devoted efforts by which I was snatched from a watery grave. I feel certain that, had your hand not been stretched forth at that awful moment, I should not now be alive to pen these lines.
Although I am but a boy, I trust that I am properly impressed with a sense of the heavy obligation under which I lie to you; and it is my sincere hope that I may hereafter convince you that the life you have saved is not a worthless one; ...

5

Time-line

	Pre-**1880s**	**1880s**	**1890s**	**1900s**	**1910s**	**1920**
		Great great grandparents were born			**Great grandparents were born**	
Important events	**1870** Alexander Graham Bell invents telephone	**1888** Dunlop invents pneumatic tyre	**1890** Moving pictures start **1896** First modern Olympic Games	**1901** Queen Victoria dies. Edward VII becomes King **1903** Wright brothers fly first plane	**1910** George V becomes King **1914–18** World War I	**1926** Gene Strike in Britain
Post and letter writing dates	**1840** First adhesive postage stamps ● Penny Post begins **1852** First ever post box set up in Jersey **1870** Postcards delivered for a halfpenny ● Post Office takes over telegram services ● Post Office issues its own plain postcards ● Education Act makes schooling compulsory up to the age of eleven **1874** Invention of the typewriter	**1883** Parcel post begins **1884** Waterman perfects a non-leaking fountain pen **1887** Horse-drawn mail vans for parcel post, brought back due to expense of sending parcels by rail	**1890** Golden Jubilee (fifty years) of Penny Post **1892** Letter cards introduced **1894** Post Office allows sending of privately printed postcards. Postcard craze begins **1897** Post Office experiments with petrol and steam driven vehicles to speed mail delivery ● Queen Victoria's Diamond Jubilee. Postal delivery guaranteed to every house in the kingdom	**1905** Conversion of horse drawn parcel vans to motorised vans begins ● Envelopes with windows introduced	**1911** Post Office takes over telephone system ● First mail carried by air – between Hendon and Windsor as part of the Coronation celebrations for George V **1912** First automatic telephone exchange set up **1919** Post Office establishes its own fleet of motor vehicles ● First regular international airmail service between London and Paris	**1927** Post Office's own undergroun railway syst opened in London. It joined most the main sorting offic with the ma line railway stations

6

This time-line shows some of the important events since your great great grandparents were children and some events and inventions which have changed the way we write and send letters.

grandparents were born		Parents were born		You were born		
1930s	1940s	1950s	1960s	1970s	1980s	1990s

1936 Edward abdicates. George VI becomes King. First television broadcasts	1941 Penicillin successfully tested	1952 Elizabeth II becomes Queen		1973 Britain enters the Common Market	1981 First successful space shuttle flight	
	1945 World War II ends					
1939 World War II starts	1947 First supersonic plane	1959 Yuri Gagarin first man in space	1969 Neil Armstrong – first man on the moon			

EIIR

	1940 Biro brothers patent the ballpoint pen	1959 Post codes first tried in Norwich	1963 International Subscriber Dialling (ISD) starts. People can make calls directly without going through the operator	1970 Datapost, a way of sending special parcels quickly, introduced	1980 Intelpost, the world's first public international facsimile mail service started	1990 150th anniversary of the Penny Post
1935 Greetings telegrams introduced. First mechanised sorting of mail			1965 onwards Mechanisation of sorting mail using post codes	1971 The last lineside apparatus used by TPOs is taken out of service		
1937 Self-sealing envelopes	1949 Last horse-drawn mail van used in London		1966 First commercial communications satellite, Early Bird put into orbit over the Atlantic Ocean	1974 Postcoding of every address in the UK is completed		
1939 Flying boats carry mail across the Atlantic			1967 Introduction of postbuses, carrying mail and people in remote areas	1979 Night airlift service starts to speed first class inland mail		
			1968 First and second class letter post begins			

Greetings

Biro

7

Correspondence

This is a selection of the kind of post which was sent in great grandma's time.

▼ Decorated notepaper was very popular for ladies' letters and invitations.

▼ Before the Penny Post, when letters were charged by the number of sheets used, people often wrote both ways across the paper to save money.

▼ To announce a death or the date of a funeral, people wrote on black-edged paper.

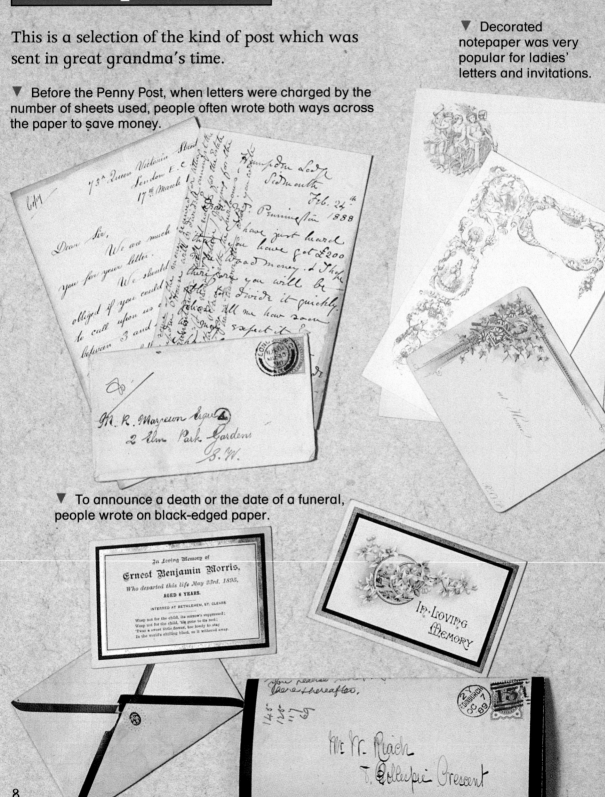

▼ Businesses often advertised their services on fancy letter headings for their bills and letters. Typewriters were invented in 1874, and by 1900, were widely in use in business

▼ The court and high society sent printed invitations like this.

▲ The first Christmas card was sent in 1843. By 1900, this had become a common custom.

Postcards

In 1870, the Post Office brought out a plain postcard, which could be sent for one halfpenny (half the price of a letter). In 1894, it allowed people to post privately printed postcards. A great craze started for sending postcards and many young ladies collected them to put into albums. By the turn of the century, postcards made up a third of the mail. In 1908 alone, 860 million postcards were sent.

Postcard firms used the new techniques for printing photographs to produce cards on all sorts of topical themes. Thomas Cook and other travel firms had recently started organising tours abroad, and it became very fashionable for well-off people to send postcards home. Businesses had postcards printed, advertising their products, and families had postcards made from photographs of themselves.

▼ You can buy many old postcards quite cheaply. Their messages and pictures can often tell you about the way people lived.

▼ The Post Office postcard of 1870. It was small, plain, and had the stamp printed on it. People wrote the address on one side and the message on the other.

▼ Birthday and Easter greetings were often sent on postcards.

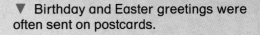

▼ Marie Studholme was a famous theatrical star in the early 1900s.

▲ A humorous card printed at a time when cars were still quite a novelty.

▲ A family photograph printed on to a postcard.

▲ A funny card advertising cheap-day fares to the seaside.

▲ A card commemorating the reign of Edward VII, who died in 1910.

▲ A holiday postcard sent from Italy in 1906.

Writing equipment

▲ Ink dried very slowly, so people used blotters like this to dry the ink and stop it from smudging.

◄ There was a choice of hundreds of nibs, often sold in very decorative boxes. Nibs could be plain or fancy, fine or broad, or shaped for a particular purpose, such as italic writing or mapping.

Edward VII, who was the king in great grandma's childhood, always used quill pens, made from feathers, which he sharpened with a penknife. Some older people also used quill pens, but most people used pens with detachable steel nibs, which were dipped into ink. Cheap pen-nib holders were made of wood; more expensive ones were made of ivory, mother-of-pearl, glass, silver or gold.

The ink was kept in an inkwell, which usually had a solid base so that it didn't spill, a lid, and a narrow neck to stop the ink from drying out and dust from getting in.

▲ The pen on the left is a folding dip pen. The pen beside it is the sort that schoolchildren used. The fountain pen on the right was filled with ink using the glass dropper.

▲ This child is writing with a dip pen. Notice the two pen wipers – one made of cloth and the other of bristles.

An advertisement for a fountain pen, ▲ in 1904. They were very expensive, so most people used dip pens.

The nibs needed frequent wiping to stop them from being eaten away by acids in the ink. Penwipers were made of fabric or, sometimes, from bristles. Many children from poor families made a living by making cheap penwipers from scraps of black cloth.

Several inventors tried making a pen with its own supply of ink, but all of their pens leaked. Lewis Waterman was the first, in 1884, to patent a successful fountain pen which never leaked. He made a fortune from his invention. By the early 1900s, there were several other popular makes of fountain pens. 13

The Penny Post

In 1890, the Post Office celebrated the Golden Jubilee (50 years) of the Penny Post. Before penny postage, the cost of sending a letter varied, depending on how far the letter was going and how many sheets of paper it was. Sending two sheets instead of one cost double the amount.

People didn't use envelopes. Instead, they folded their letters and sealed them with wax or a wafer.

The postage was usually paid by the person who received the letter. Sometimes, people wouldn't, or couldn't, pay. Letters were only delivered to houses in big towns and deliveries were slow, because the letter-carriers had to knock and collect the money for postage.

▼ The Penny Black, the first postage stamp ever issued. Since Britain was the first to use stamps, it is the only country which does not have its name printed on them.

▲ Post marks commemorating the Jubilee of the Penny Post.

◄ Wafers were made of a mixture of flour, gum and colouring. They were licked and stuck on to letters or envelopes, as this girl is doing.

In 1840, Rowland Hill introduced a new system of postage, based on weight. The cost of a sending a letter anywhere in the country, however far, was one penny. The sender paid for the postage by buying a stamp and sticking it on the letter.

The Penny Post was very popular. It meant that many more people could afford to send letters. People were encouraged to put letter boxes in their doors for letters to be delivered. Post boxes were built for people to post their letters. In London, there were only six post boxes in 1855; by 1900, there were over thirty thousand!

At first, deliveries were made only to major towns but, by the end of the century, there was a regular delivery to even the most remote villages.

By Command of the Postmaster General.

NOTICE to the PUBLIC.

Rapid Delivery of Letters.

GENERAL POST OFFICE,
May. 1849.

The Postmaster General is desirous of calling attention to the greater rapidity of delivery which would obviously be consequent on the general adoption of *Street-door Letter Boxes, or Slits*, in private dwelling houses, and indeed wherever the Postman is at present kept waiting.

He hopes that householders will not object to the means by which, at a very moderate expense, they may secure so desirable an advantage to themselves, to their neighbours, and to the Public Service.

▲ The Post Office issued this notice encouraging people to put letter boxes in their doors.

▼ This child is trying out some sealing wax. He drips a blob of wax on to the envelope and presses an engraved seal on to it. Wealthy people often had their own personal seals.

The parcel post

In 1883, the Post Office started a parcel post for every town and village in the country. Every post office had to be refitted for sorting parcels and provided with scales and new hand-stamps for cancelling the stamps.

Modern post offices usually have a special counter with large scales and a wide hatch for handing parcels through. The clerks often use hand-stamps to cancel the stamps before the parcels are sent. When you next visit your local post office, ask if you can have a look at a hand-stamp.

◀ A parcel coach, 1900. The mail was protected by a guard, who was armed with a revolver and a sword bayonet. He sorted the mail inside the coach as it travelled.

▼ A parcel post tricycle.

Parcels, in 1883, were packed in large wicker baskets for transporting from town to town. Some parcels were sent by rail, but since this was expensive, new road vehicles were made to carry them. The first vans were horse drawn but, by 1905, most vehicles were motorised and the heavy baskets had been replaced by lighter sacks.

The letter carriers' walks had to be changed, so that they did not have too heavy a load to carry. They were given handcarts or bicycles with large baskets in front, to make their deliveries easier. Now they no longer only carried letters, they were given a new name – postmen.

◀ An early motor mail van.

▼ Find out what you can send by parcel post now and whether there is any weight limit.

Sending a letter

◄ Victorian post boxes are hexagonal, fluted or cylindrical shaped. Compare them with the shapes of modern post boxes.

▼ In Britain, in 1900, 2000 million letters, 400 million postcards and 700 million printed papers were sent through the post.

The postal system in great grandma's day was very efficient. By 1908, London had twelve daily deliveries and most big cities had at least six. Edith Hall describes how her family kept in daily touch by post:

'My grandmother would send us a card each evening which we received by the first delivery the next morning. She would then receive our reply card the same evening. If one lived in the same town as one's correspondent, an early morning posted card would be delivered at twelve mid-day the same day and a reply card, if sent immediately, would be received the same afternoon.'

How many deliveries do you have?

SECOND CLASS

IMPORTANT NOTICE
TO AVOID DELAY
PLEASE POST
IN THE
PROPER BOXES

Collections

POST IN THE RIGHT BOX
This box now has an aperture for First Class and foreign mail and one for Second Class. Please post in the correct aperture to avoid delay.

Collections

POST OFFICE

ER

◄ Edwardian post boxes are all cylindrical. Some are double-width.

Postmen collected letters from the post boxes several times a day, just as postmen still do today. See if you can find an old post box in your area. Many post boxes from great grandma's day are still being used.

Victorian post boxes are marked VR. This stands for Victoria Regina, meaning Queen Victoria. Edwardian post boxes are marked ER VII. This stands for Eduardus Rex VII, which is Latin for King Edward VII.

▲ Modern post boxes have ER II on them. What does this stand for?

19

Sorting the post

▲ Hundreds of sorters were employed in big post offices. Extra men, who had other daytime jobs, helped sort the early morning delivery and last despatch mail.

▲ Stamps and postmarks used in the time of Edward VII.

The letters were taken to the post office, where they were emptied on to a big table. Clerks 'faced' the letters, putting the stamps all facing the same way, so that it was easier to cancel them. The stamps were cancelled by hand with a postmark, which showed the date, time and place where the letters had been posted. Letters are still marked with a postmark, but now this is normally done by machine.

Sorters divided the stamped letters into pigeon holes for different parts of the country. Other sorters further divided the letters into individual towns. The post for each town was put into mail bags, which were labelled and sealed. The bags were taken to railway stations or loaded on to vans and sent to different towns.

At their destination, the letters were taken to the local post office and sorted into streets. Postmen sorted their own pile into the right order for their 'walk', or delivery round.

To make sorting easier, when the amount of mail increased after the Penny Post, London was divided into postal districts. Later, other big towns did the same. In the 1890s, there was a campaign to alter the names of any streets in a district which shared the same name, as that caused confusion for sorters.

If you live in a town, contact your Public Records Office and ask if you can look at the street or city directories from around this time. Did the streets in your neighbourhood change names? Can you find any other evidence of street names being changed at this time?

▲ The carved street sign has no postal district, so it must be earlier than 1856, when the postal district system was introduced. The districts were numbered in 1917 to make sorting even easier.

▲ Horse-drawn mail vans carried mail to and from railway stations, and to other post offices in the same town. Motorised vans were introduced in 1905.

▲ Part of a letter dated 28 July 1892 from the London County Council to the Postmaster General. The Council and the Post Office disagreed on how many streets had the same names and needed to be renamed.

21

Travelling Post Offices

By 1900, major towns were linked by the railways and most letters were sent by train. The trains had a specially designed carriage, called a Travelling Post Office (TPO for short), with pigeon holes for sorting the mail which was picked up en route.

Mail bags could be picked up and off-loaded while the train was moving. Fixed to the side of the carriage was an apparatus for dropping bags, and a large net for collecting new ones. Along the route, mail bags were hung on tall posts to be scooped up in the net as the train sped past. The mail being dropped off the train was caught by a net at the side of the track.

▲ The interior of a TPO in 1900.

▼ The exterior of a TPO, showing the collection net and the apparatus for dropping the mail bags.

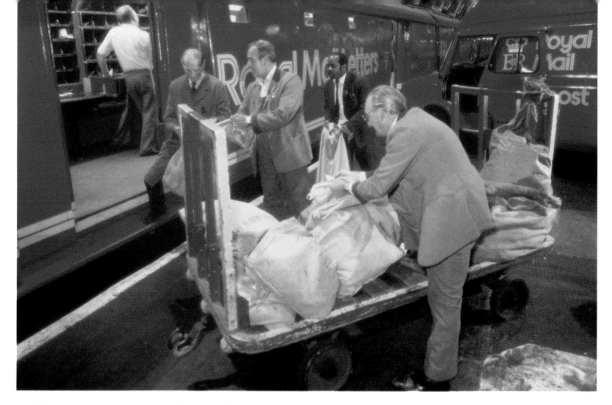

▲ These postmen are loading mail on to a modern night mail train.

▼ Hanging up a mail bag for collection by TPO.

A great deal of post still travels around Britain by train. There are modern TPOs on some of the lines and long-distance night mail trains, which don't carry passengers or pick up post en route. You could go to your local station and find out how often mail is loaded and delivered there. See if anyone there remembers the old TPO system.

Country post offices

In the country, the post office was often part of a village store or a room set aside in a house. In 1900, Flora Thompson worked in a post office, attached to a smithy. It was:

'A long, low white house which might have been . . . an ordinary cottage . . . but for a scarlet-painted letter-box let into the wall beneath a window at one end. Over the window was a painted board which informed the public that the building was CANDLEFORD GREEN POST AND TELEGRAPHIC OFFICE.'

The mail was brought from the nearest town by foot, cart, or by a postman on a horse, which he provided himself, in return for a weekly sum from the post office. Postmen without a horse were expected to walk 25 km a day, whatever the weather, carrying a 15 kg load. They were given a boot allowance, because they walked so much!

▼ A country post office which was part of a village store. Even today, many village stores house a small post office.

Usually, there was only one delivery a day to people's homes. In the afternoon, people came to the post office to collect any other mail. Wealthy families had private postbags, which they would arrange to have carried to and from the post office.

The working hours were long, as Flora describes:

'From the arrival of the seven o'clock morning mail till the office closed at night (at eight o'clock) ... and Sunday not entirely free, for there was a Sunday morning delivery of letters and an outward mail to be made up in the evening.'

But as the Post Office was not busy all the time:

'... Meals could be taken in comparative peace, reading or knitting was possible ... and there were opportunities of getting out into the fresh air.'

▲ Bicycles were introduced by 1900. The postman's route was extended to 35 km a day with a load of 22 kg. Shelters were built for postmen to eat and rest in, so that they weren't tempted to spend too long in the pub instead.

◀ You can find early post boxes set into the wall of some old country cottages.

◀ Some country postal workers still deliver letters by bicycle. This postwoman cycles 240 km a week.

Overseas mail

By the beginning of this century, Britain governed a huge number of countries, including India, parts of Africa, Hong Kong and the West Indies. These countries were called British Colonies. The British Government needed to keep in constant touch with its officials overseas, so a frequent, reliable and speedy postal service was vital.

In 1898, it was agreed that there should be a penny post rate for letters sent to any British colony (except Australia, New Zealand and The Cape). This meant that, for only a penny, a letter could be sent half way round the world to a colony; to send a letter to France cost double.

▲ This map shows (in pink) the extent of the British Empire in 1900, and the shipping routes for the mail.

MAIL FLAG

An ocean steamer which carried mail across the Atlantic (illustration from an Edwardian children's book).

◀ This postcard was sent round the world to mark the Golden Jubilee of the Penny Post in 1890. It took 107 days to travel from England, via Gibraltar, Egypt, Aden, India, Hong Kong, Japan, America and Canada, back to its sender.

There were no aeroplanes in 1900. The Post Office gave a yearly payment to shipping companies to carry the post. Overseas mail went by steamship and took a long time. It took two weeks, for example, for a letter to reach Bombay, in India, and a month for one to reach Australia.

Mail was carried across the Atlantic in big passenger ships. Mail for India and the Far East was carried in fast mail ships, called packet ships, which also took passengers. In the event of a shipwreck, the shipping companies were instructed to save the mail first and the passengers afterwards!

27

Then and now

▲ Post offices in large towns were usually imposing buildings like this one.

In some big towns, you will still be able to see grand old post offices built around the turn of the century. If you find one, look for the date when it was built. There may be a sign on the outside. In your great grandma's day, the inside of a large post office would probably have looked a bit like the picture above. If you are able to visit one, look for clues to show you how it was used.

Find out when your local post office was built. If it was built in the last fifty years, find out whether there was an earlier post office there, or in a different spot.

In 1900, you could send a letter, a book, a newspaper or a parcel by post. The Post Office sold stamps, postcards, lettercards,

money orders and postal orders. It also issued licences for dogs, guns, private brewers, male servants (including gardeners), carriages, cars and marriages. It ran an Express Delivery service for urgent letters and a Post Restante system, where post could be called for.

It was also a savings bank, sold insurance policies and operated telephone and telegraph services.

Since great grandma's time, there have been many changes in the Post Office, but you may be surprised to discover how much is still the same. Find out which of these services the Post Office still provides and if it offers any new ones.

▲ This sign was on the front of a post office built in great grandma's day. See what old signs you can find.

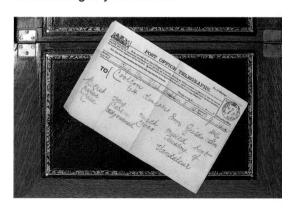

▲ A telegram sent in 1888.   29

How to find out more

Start here	To find out about . . .	Who will have . . .
Old people	How people wrote and sent letters and cards	Memories about writing and receiving letters and cards. Old letters, postcards, bills and other documents. Stamp collections. Writing equipment, such as pens, inkwells, blotters, writing cases etc.
• Junk shops • Second-hand bookshops • Stamp shops	Old things to buy	• Old postcards, stamps, stationery, old magazines and advertisements • Old books • Stamps of different periods
Local museums	Old things to look at and possibly to handle	Show case displays of equipment and ephemera. Handling collections of objects you can touch and try out. Reconstructions – old objects gathered from different places and put together in a setting to give the feeling of how they would have been originally
Local library	• Loan collections • Reference collections • Schools loan collections • Local studies collections • Information desk	• Books to borrow • Books, back copies of magazines and newspapers to consult there • Big libraries sometimes have a special section for schools • Local documents and possibly a photograph collection of local people, buildings and places. Oral history tapes of local people • Useful addresses and additional information on how you can further your research
The Post Office	Useful information about the modern Post Office and its history	Details about the Stamp Bug Club. Information about visits. Information about educational packs about the Post Office. Stamps, postcards and forms for other modern post services

Who can tell you more?

They can. Use a tape recorder for recording their memories. Handle anything they show you with great care and if they lend you something, label it with their name and keep it somewhere safe

Specialist shopkeepers are usually very enthusiastic and knowledgeable about their stock. They may also be able to give you further contacts and addresses

The curator or the museum's education officer. Many museums also have a bookshop and a notice board where it would be worth looking for further information

● The librarian
● Ask to see a museum's guide in the library if you don't live near a museum with a relevant collection

● Ask for the name of the secretary of the local history society for local information

The Post Office educational and information service (for the address, see under *Other useful addresses*)

Places to visit

Abbey House, Kirkstall, Leeds, West Yorkshire. Tel: 0532 755821 (reconstructed stationer's shop window and artefacts.)
Bath Postal Museum, 8 Broad Street, Bath, Avon BA1 5LJ. Tel: 0225 60333 (Displays about postal history.)
Beamish, North of England Open Air Museum, Beamish Hall, Stanley, Co. Durham. Tel: 0207 231811 (Stationer's shop and printer's workshop.)
Birmingham Museum of Science and Industry, Newhall Street, Birmingham B3 1RZ. Tel: 021–236 1022 (The Charles Turner collection of writing implements.)
Bruce Castle Museum, Lordship Lane, London N17 8NU. Tel: 01–808 8722 (Displays about early postal history.)
Gloucester Folk Museum, 99–103 Westgate Street, Gloucester GL1 2PG. Tel: 0452 26467 (Writing equipment)
Mount Pleasant Letter District Office, London EC1A 1BB. (Address letters to the District Head Postmaster, Room 414, Public Office Block). (Organises visits to see the mechanised letter sorting office and the Post Office underground railway. Visits last 1½ hours. Parties up to 30 in number.)
National Postal Museum, King Edward Building, King Edward Street, London EC1A 1LP. Tel: 01–239 5420 (One of the largest stamp collections in the world. Also stamp cancelling machines, stamp boxes, postmark dies and letter boxes. Sales counter with postcards, books and copies of the British Philatelic Bulletin (published monthly). (School parties welcome.)
Red House Museum, Quay Road, Christchurch, Dorset BH23 1BU. Tel: 0202 482860 (Collection of writing implements.)
Rexel Cumberland Pencil Museum, The Cumberland Pencil Co. Ltd., Southey Works, Greta Bridge, Keswick, Cumbria CA12 5NG. Tel: 07687 73626 (History of pencil making, brass rubbing, children's drawing corner. School parties welcome.)
Royston Museum, Lower King Street, Herts. Tel: 0763 42587 (Small postal history collection.)
Telecom Technology Showcase, 135 Queen Victoria Street, London EC4 4AT. Tel: 01–248 7447 (History of telecommunications.)

Other useful addresses:

British Philatelic Bureau, 20 Brandon Street, Edinburgh EH3 5TT.
Stanley Gibbons, stamp dealers, 399 Strand, London WC2R 0LX. Tel: 01–836 8444
Stanley Gibbons Publications, Parkside, Ringwood, Hants, BH24 3SH. (stamp catalogues.)
Letter Box Study Group, Secretary: Sally Jones, 43 Miall Road, Hall Green, Birmingham BS28 9BS. (Information and listings about old post boxes.)

Picture Postcard Monthly (magazine), 15 Debdale Lane, Keyworth, Nottingham NG12 5HT. Tel: 06077 4079 (Informative articles on collecting old postcards, as well as addresses of postcard shops and notice of postcard and stamp fairs.)
Postcard Association, 6 Wimpole Street, London W1M 8AS. Tel: 01–637 7692
Post Office Archives, Freeling House, 23 Glasshill Street, London SE1 0BQ. Tel: 01–261 1145 (Provides free information sheets on various aspects of the history of the Post Office; for example: pillar boxes, railways and the post office, letter and parcel post, postal uniforms, postal districts and the development of road transport.)

Post Office Educational and Information Services, Public Relations Unit, Royal Mail House, 29 Wellington Street, Leeds LS1 1DA. (Provides educational material on request for primary, middle and secondary schools.)
The Stamp Bug Club, FREEPOST, PO Box 109, Penn, High Wycombe, Buckinghamshire, HP10 8BR. (A club set up by the Post Office for young stamp collectors. Members receive a magazine, *Stamp Bug News*, six times a year, which contains stamp collecting news, competitions and swap pages.)
The Writing Equipment Society. Information from Maureen Greenland, 4 Greystones Grange Crescent, Sheffield S11 7JL.

Index